Usborne

Big Picture Book
Dinosaurs

Laura Cowan

Illustrated by Gianluca Foli

Designed by Zoe Wray

Expert: Dr. Darren Naish, University of Southampton

Usborne Quicklinks

For links to websites where you can watch video clips
about dinosaurs and learn how to say all the names in this book, go to

www.usborne.com/quicklinks and type in the keywords, 'big picture dinosaurs'.

We recommend that children are supervised while using the internet.
Please follow the internet safety guidelines at the Usborne Quicklinks website.

Contents

Each big picture scene in this book shows dinosaurs that lived together during the same period.

Hello, dinosaurs!

Millions and millions of years ago, long before there were people, the world belonged to creatures unlike any you've ever seen. Many of these were DINOSAURS. Millions of years is SUCH a long time, it's hard to imagine. But try.

At first, there was NOTHING living on Earth. No plants. No animals. Just rocks.

POP

From the nothing, slowly, slowly, over millions and millions and MILLIONS of years, living things grew.

SPLOSH

TIKTAALIK

JELLYFISH

SPLAT

DIMETRODON

The names of animals that are NOT DINOSAURS are shown like this.

About 200 million years ago, the first types of dinosaurs appeared.

Hello, dinosaur!

There were plants, such as ferns, but no flowers.

COELOPHYSIS

The names of different types of dinosaur are shown like this.

Most of the first dinosaurs were only the size of a big dog or a cow. But later dinosaurs came in all different shapes and sizes.

ARRRRP

Some were **feathery** and some were **furry**. Some were **scaly**, too.

Some had **big** heads, some had big tails, and some had **jagged teeth** and **sharp claws**.

Some were tiny but some were **BIGGER** than ANY animal EVER to walk the earth.

STAURIKOSAURUS

This was the world of the dinosaurs.

RIOJASAURUS

These gentle giants lived together peacefully – there was lots of food for everyone.

DIPLODOCUS

ORNITHOLESTES

Gentle giants

Lots of dinosaurs were big and slow. These kinds only ate plants, but still grew as big as a BUS or a HOUSE. They plodded around in groups called herds.

CAMPTOSAURUS

Ornitholestes was not like the giant dinosaurs. It ate MEAT.

LOOK OUT, CAMPTOSAURUS – Ornitholestes wants to eat you!

NIP, NIP!

Stumpy front legs for crouching close to the plants it ate

Strong back legs for running

Long neck to reach
high up for food

Swoosh!
Swoosh!

When the dinosaurs had eaten
all the food in one place, they
would move to another.

Bony plates stopped
other dinosaurs from
eating Stegosaurus.

THWACK
THWACK

Spiked tail for
swiping at enemies
or annoying
little dinos

STEGOSAURUS

STOP BITING
MY TAIL, TINY
DINOSAUR!

Dinosaur eats dinosaur

Some dinosaurs didn't eat plants and they didn't live in herds. Some dinosaurs were scarier than the rest – they ate OTHER DINOSAURS.

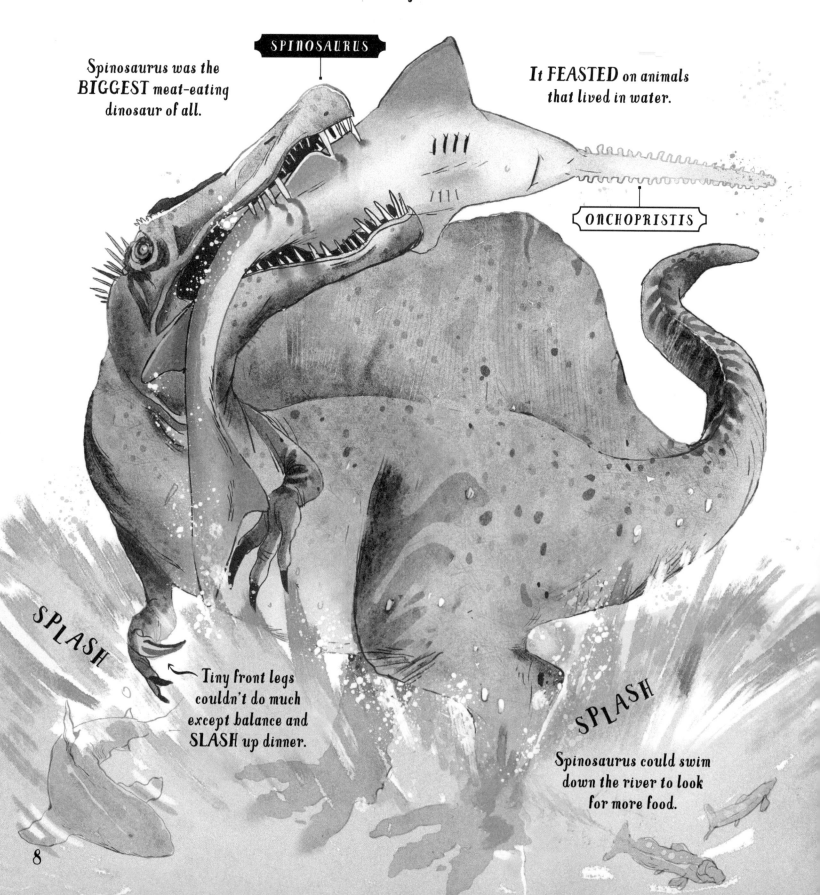

Spinosaurus was the BIGGEST meat-eating dinosaur of all.

SPINOSAURUS

It FEASTED on animals that lived in water.

ONCHOPRISTIS

SPLASH

Tiny front legs couldn't do much except balance and SLASH up dinner.

SPLASH

Spinosaurus could swim down the river to look for more food.

Tyrannosaurus rex – or T.rex for short – was KING of the dinosaurs.
Other dinosaurs were bigger, but T.rex was SCARIER. Other dinosaurs ran away from T.rex.

TYRANNOSAURUS REX

EDMONTOSAURUS

WERGH

Why? Because T.rex ate EVERYTHING. Sometimes it even ate OTHER T.REXES.

This little dinosaur is
nicknamed the 'chicken
from hell' because it looked
like the scariest chicken
EVER.

RAAAAAAAR

ANZU

Uh-oh, is Anzu going to
be GOBBLED UP?

Tiny dinosaurs

Lots of dinosaurs weren't big at all. They were the size of pigeons. They weren't scary either – some were covered in shiny feathers.

Microraptor used its tail to change direction in the air.

NEOOOOW

Its wings were for gliding and floating on gusts of wind.

Sometimes Microraptor feathers looked black.

Sometimes they shimmered purple, blue and green.

SWOOSH!

IS THAT A BUTTERFLY?

NO, IT ONLY **LOOKS LIKE** A BUTTERFLY.

Kalligramma was an insect that lived over 100 million years ago.

FLITTER FLUTTER

KALLIGRAMMA

Kalligramma flapped its wings and flew up or down or around.

11

Massive Dinosaur FIGHT!

Argentinosaurus was one of the BIGGEST dinosaurs EVER. Giganotosaurus looked tiny next to Argentinosaurus, but it was HUGE too. And HUNGRY for dinosaur meat...

GIGANOTOSAURUS

SNARL
SNARL

Its teeth weren't good for biting other dinosaurs – they were for chewing plants.

FIGHT!

Giganotosaurus had sharp teeth and claws for slashing – and it fought in packs.

From its nose to the tip of its tail, Argentinosaurus was as long as three buses back to back.

WHOOSH

Argentinosaurus fought back using its HUGE tail and STRONG legs.

RRRARRRR

SNAP
SNAP

FIGHT!

Could a Giganotosaurus pack take down the biggest dinosaur ever? They're going to try...

PSSSSST! These dinos might not look big next to Argentinosaurus, but look on pages 30-31 and you will see how MASSIVE they really were...

Blending in

Some dinosaurs were very good at hiding – from the animals hunting them... and the things they hunted.

These little dinosaurs were striped like tigers. Stripes helped Sinornithosaurus blend in with the shadows of branches and STRIPES of sunlight.

SINORNITHOSAURUS

RRRRR!

Sinornithosaurus didn't sleep at night and it didn't sleep in the day. Instead, it had little naps whenever it was tired.

NNNNN

THESE INSECTS
WOULD BE A
TASTY MEAL!

BOO

Sinornithosaurus lurked
in between the trees
where insects couldn't
see it and then...
HELLO, LUNCH!

How many Sinornithosaurus
can you spot?

Standing out

Some dinosaurs were good at hiding, but others did the opposite.
They stood out to SCARE AWAY enemies, or to SHOW OFF to friends.

Zhenyuanlong looked like a big bird,
but it couldn't fly.

ZHENYUANLONG

Bright feathers
said to other male
Zhenyuanlongs,
GO AWAY,
THIS IS MY LAND.

Feathers kept
these dinosaurs
nice and warm.

Bright feathers on male Zhenyuanlongs
said to females,
HEY, COME ON OVER.

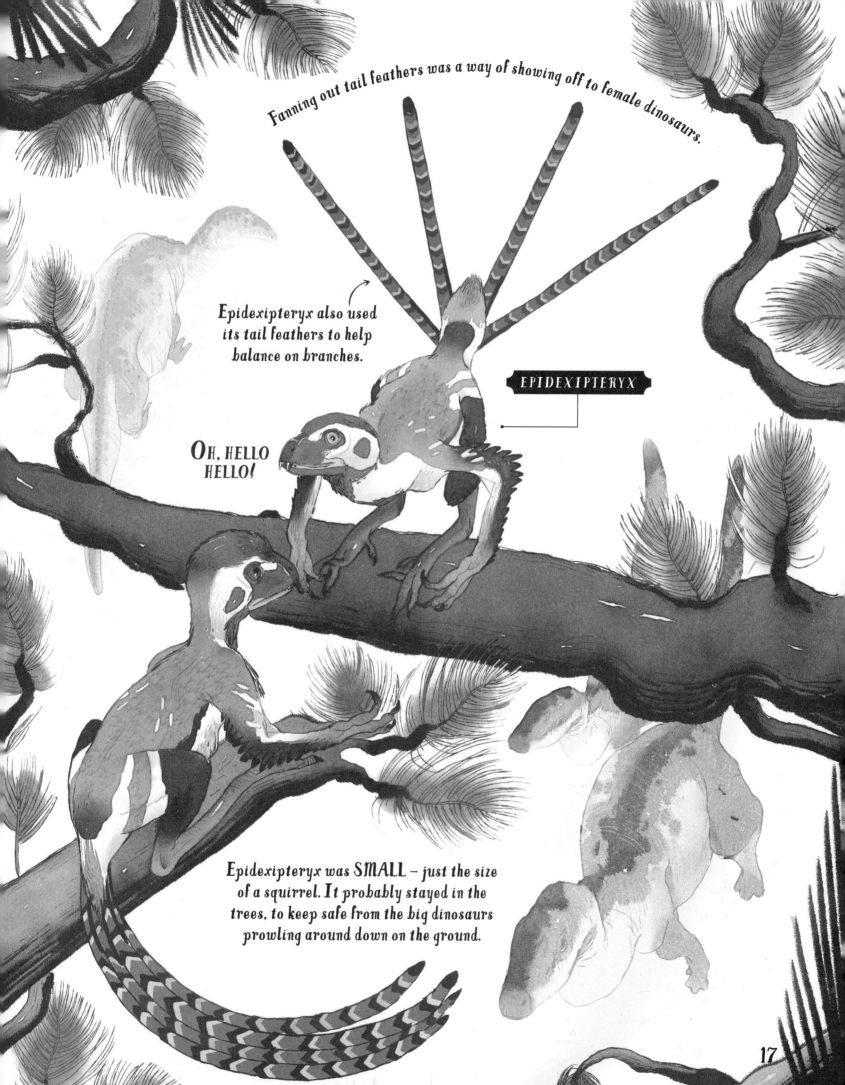

Fanning out tail feathers was a way of showing off to female dinosaurs.

Epidexipteryx also used its tail feathers to help balance on branches.

EPIDEXIPTERYX

OH, HELLO HELLO!

Epidexipteryx was SMALL – just the size of a squirrel. It probably stayed in the trees, to keep safe from the big dinosaurs prowling around down on the ground.

Babies

Where did baby dinosaurs come from?
Well, they started life inside
surprisingly small eggs...

MAIASAURA

A female Maiasaura laid 30 or 40 eggs at once.
Each egg was about the size of a big orange.

Maiasaura lined their nests
with leaves and plants to
keep the eggs warm.

A baby dinosaur
grew inside each egg.

When can I
come out of
my shell?

CRRRRRRRRRACK

TAP-TAP

Months and
months later,
the shells started
to crack...

It was hard being a baby dinosaur. Baby dinosaurs were very small and the world was very big. But Maiasaura lived in herds and they helped each other.

Maiasaura looked after its little babies. It fed them bits of plant, and tried to keep them safe.

PEEP

PEEP

PEEP

PEEP

PEEP

...and babies hatched out of the eggs.

TAP-TAP

PEEP

24-hour desert dinos

Some dinosaurs lived in deserts. Deserts 80 million years ago were like deserts today – except for the dinosaurs.

There's not much to eat in deserts – there aren't as many plants as in other places, just lots of dust. During the daytime, the sun is HOT.

Some dinosaurs dozed during the day. It was too hot for them to move.

PROTOCERATOPS

ZZZZZZ

Other dinosaurs didn't mind heat – they were the ones that moved very... SLOWLY.

PINACOSAURUS

The afternoon was SLEEPY TIME for Protoceratops. Food time was later.

STOMP

STOMP

STOMP

CRRRRUNCH

When the sun goes down, the desert cools. Dinosaurs that slept during the day woke up and looked for food at night. For them, it was HUNTING TIME.

Velociraptor and Mononykus had HUGE eyes.

MONONYKUS

HUGE eyes were ALL THE BETTER for seeing things in the dark.

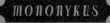

PROTOCERATOPS

REOWWWWWW

VELOCIRAPTOR

WATCH OUT PROTOCERATOPS!

EEK

Velociraptor could see better and move faster than Protoceratops.

mmmmmmmm?

Flight of the pterosaurs

Up in the sky there were **NO** dinosaurs at all. But there were all kinds of amazing flying creatures called pterosaurs.

CROUCH!

VAULT!

TAKE OFF!

TROPEOGNATHUS

Fuzzy hairs called pycnofibres, kept pterosaurs' bodies cosy.

The water had lots of fish – food for pterosaurs.

TAPEJARA

TUPUXUARA

Pterosaurs had light, hollow bones filled with air, so they could float in the sky.

Tupuxuara had a big bony crest on its head. But what was it for?

Letting out heat to keep cool?

Steering through the sky?

So they could show off?

No one knows... yet.

THALASSODROMEUS

Yum yum, delicious baby dinosaurs!

WATCH OUT, PTEROSAURS! CROCODILE ALERT!

SNAP! SNAP!

Sea beasts

Dinosaurs didn't live in the sea either.
But there were lots of other creatures
that were just as BIG and SCARY
as the ones on land.

Sharks might seem huge and
dangerous, but these ones were
like fluffy kittens compared
to STYXOSAURUS.

PTERANODON

STYXOSAURUS

AMMONITE

SQUALICORAX

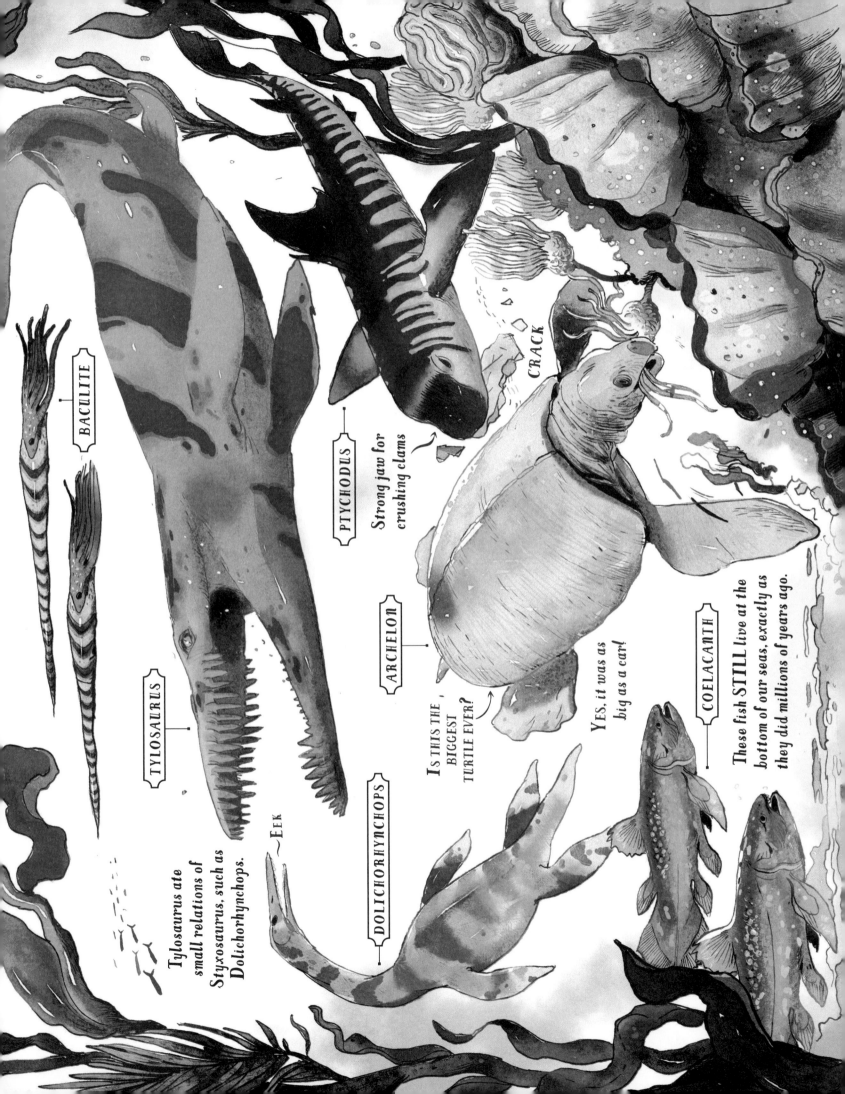

BACULITE

PTYCHODUS
Strong jaw for crushing clams

CRACK

TYLOSAURUS

Tylosaurus ate small relations of Styxosaurus, such as Dolichorhynchops.

Eek

DOLICHORHYNCHOPS

ARCHELON

IS THIS THE BIGGEST TURTLE EVER?

YES, it was as big as a car!

COELACANTH

These fish STILL live at the bottom of our seas, exactly as they did millions of years ago.

Goodbye, dinosaurs!

Dinosaurs lived on Earth for more than 150 million years.
but they don't any more. What happened to them?

BANG

PEOOOOOW

BOOM

Did lots of volcanoes erupt at once?
Spewing ash and soot and molten
lava all over the planet?

ROAAAAAAAAAAAAAAAAAAAAAAR

WAAAAAAAAAA

Did it get too hot?   Or too cold?

BRRRRRRRRR

HU HU
HU HU
HU

Any of these things might have happened.
But then, one day, a rock
AS BIG AS A CITY fell from space.

The ground
shook and broke
into pieces.

Dust shot
into the sky.

WHOOOOOOOOOSH

BOOooom

There was no light,
or warmth. Plants
on the land died.

All the pterosaurs died.
Lots of animals and sea
creatures died.

All the dinosaurs died too –
but they didn't all disappear.
At least, NOT QUITE...

Goodbye forever?

New plants and animals came along.
Millions and millions of years later, people came along, too.
But lots of things are still left from dinosaur times.

These things are called FOSSILS. They are
the traces of living plants or animals
from dinosaur times.

HUGE dinosaur
footprints

This is a fossil of an ammonite.
It lived in the sea in dinosaur times.

Massive
fossil bone

A fossil of a whole nest of dinosaur eggs and the babies inside

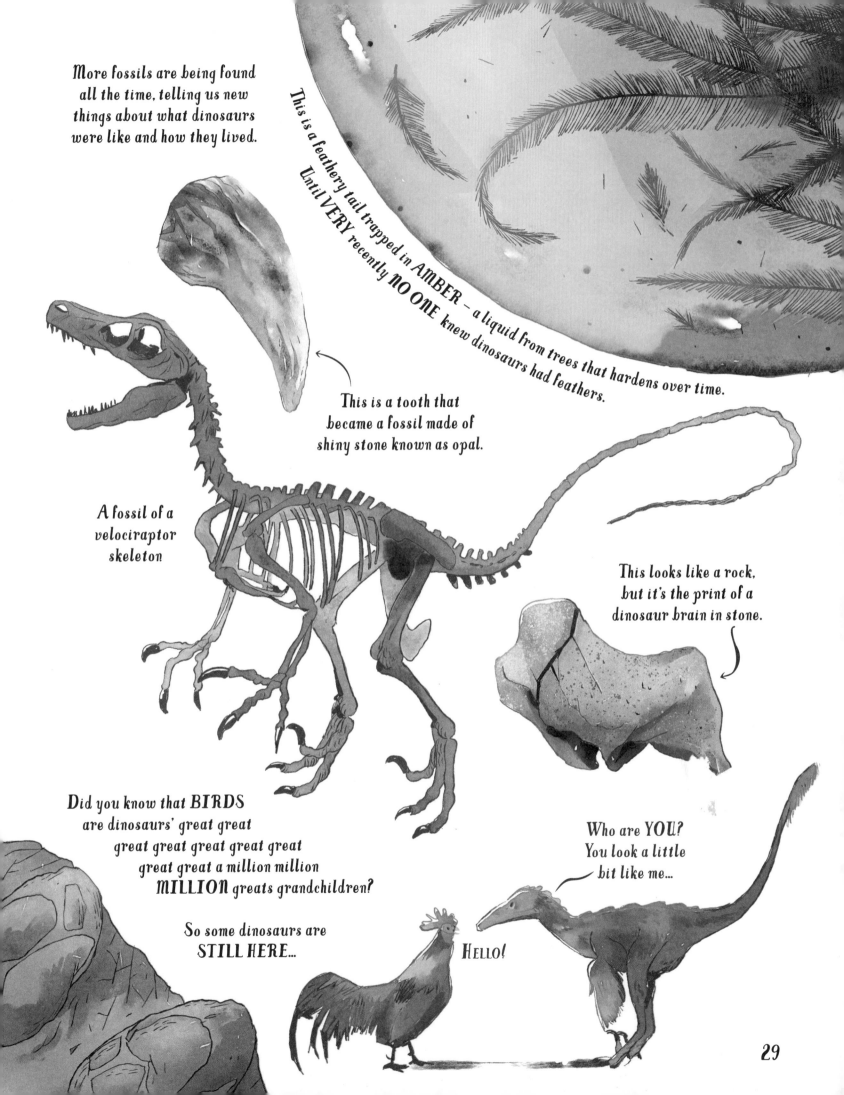

More fossils are being found all the time, telling us new things about what dinosaurs were like and how they lived.

This is a feathery tail trapped in AMBER – a liquid from trees that hardens over time. Until VERY recently NO ONE knew dinosaurs had feathers.

This is a tooth that became a fossil made of shiny stone known as opal.

A fossil of a velociraptor skeleton

This looks like a rock, but it's the print of a dinosaur brain in stone.

Did you know that BIRDS are dinosaurs' great great great great great great great great great great a million million MILLION greats grandchildren?

So some dinosaurs are STILL HERE...

Who are YOU? You look a little bit like me...

HELLO!

Roaarrr

TYRANNOSAURUS REX

Zooooom

TUPUXUARA

STEGOSAURUS

Hmmph

ARGENTINOSAURUS

BIG
and small

The dinosaurs in this book were all
different sizes. Compare them here.
How big was little Microraptor? Or
ENORMOUS ARGENTINOSAURUS?

RIOJASAURUS

MICRORAPTOR

HUMAN

ANZU

BRONTOSAURUS

Grrrrr

COELOPHYSIS

SINORNITHOSAURUS

ZHENYUANLONG

PROTOCERATOPS

Peep Peep

Snuffle snuffle

GIGANOTOSAURUS

EPIDEXIPTERYX

MAIASAURA

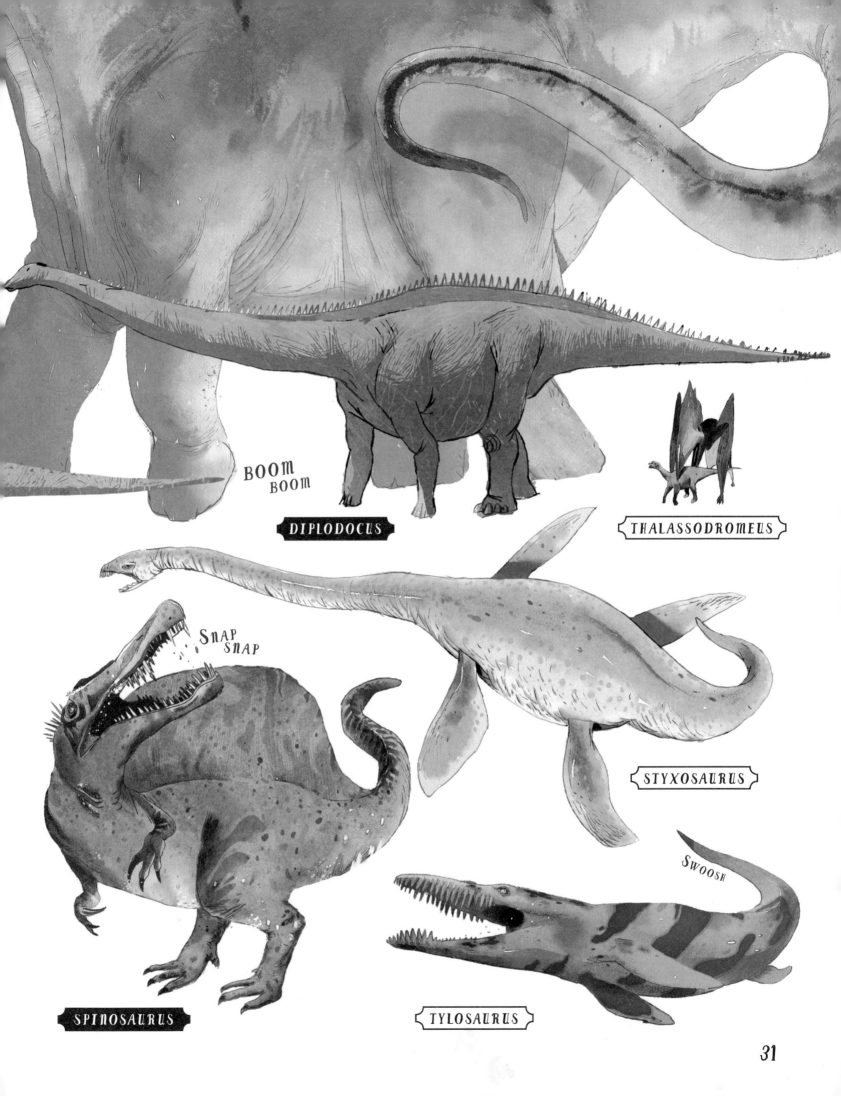

BOOM
BOOM

DIPLODOCUS

THALASSODROMEUS

SNAP
SNAP

STYXOSAURUS

SPINOSAURUS

SWOOSH

TYLOSAURUS

Index

Edited by Ruth Brocklehurst
Digital retouching and additional illustration by John Russell